W9-AAD-605

RAPTORS!
EAGLES

Rosemary Jennings

PowerKiDS
press.

New York

Published in 2016 by The Rosen Publishing Group, Inc.
29 East 21st Street, New York, NY 10010

First Edition

Editor: Sarah Machajewski
Book Design: Mickey Harmon

Photo Credits: Cover series logo Elena Paletskaya/Shutterstock.com; cover, pp. 3–6, 8, 10, 12, 14–16, 18, 20–24 (border texture, fact box) Picsfive/Shutterstock.com; cover (background scene) archana bhartia/Shutterstock.com; cover (eagle perched) Richard Lowthian/Shutterstock.com; cover, pp. 7, 13 (eagle flying) Sekar B/Shutterstock.com; p. 5 rck_593/Shutterstock.com; p. 7 (inset) Peter Wey/Shutterstock.com; p. 9 (inset) Robert Palmer/Shutterstock.com; p. 9 (main) Andy Dean Photography/Shutterstock.com; p. 11 (main) Tracing Tea/Shutterstock.com; p. 11 (inset) Igor Kovalenko/Shutterstock.com; p. 13 (golden eagle flying) Juha Niemi/Shutterstock.com; p. 15 Wild Art/Shutterstock.com; p. 17 VYACHESLAV OSELEDKO/AFP/Getty Images; p. 19 (main) Jeffery B. Banke/Shutterstock.com; p. 19 (inset) Roberta Olenick/All Canada Photos/Getty Images; p. 21 Number One/Shutterstock.com; p. 22 Phillip Rubino/Shutterstock.com.

Cataloging-in-Publication Data

Jennings, Rosemary.
Eagles / by Rosemary Jennings.
p. cm. — (Raptors!)
Includes index.
ISBN 978-1-5081-4240-9 (pbk.)
ISBN 978-1-5081-4241-6 (6-pack)
ISBN 978-1-5081-4242-3 (library binding)
1. Eagles — Juvenile literature. I. Jennings, Rosemary. II. Title.
QL696.F32 J46 2016
598.9'42—d23

Manufactured in the United States of America

CPSIA Compliance Information: Batch #BW16PK: For Further Information contact Rosen Publishing, New York, New York at 1-800-237-9932

Contents

Top of the Food Chain

In 1782, the bald eagle became the national symbol of the United States. The bald eagle may be the most familiar eagle, but there are about 60 species, or kinds, of eagles in the world. Though they have differences, all eagles have one important thing in common—they're raptors.

Eagles are large **birds of prey**. With their **keen** eyes, sharp claws, and powerful wings, eagles have no problem holding their place at the top of the food chain.

This bald eagle searches for prey from a treetop. Prey is an animal hunted by other animals for food.

RAPTOR FACTOR

Eagles are one of the largest raptors. Only some kinds of buzzards are larger.

The Raptor Family

What is a raptor? A raptor is a special kind of bird. Eagles, owls, hawks, vultures, buzzards, and falcons belong to this family. Raptors have all the features you think of when you think of birds, such as wings and feathers. But there are some features that set them apart from other birds.

Raptors are carnivores. That means they only eat meat. Raptors also have a hooked beak, sharp claws called talons, and good eyesight and hearing. These features help them do what they do best—hunt.

Eagles use their eyes, ears, feet, and beak to help them as they hunt.

good eyesight

hooked beak

feathers

sharp talons

7

Where Eagles Fly

Eagles are one of the most recognizable raptors. They're members of the bird family called Accipitridae, which also includes hawks. There are 250 species within this family. Eagles live all over the world, but most species are found in Europe and Asia. Nine species live in Central America and South America, and three species live in Australia.

Only two eagle species live in the United States and Canada. They're the bald eagle and the golden eagle. This book will focus on these eagle species.

RAPTOR FACTOR

Bald eagles are most common in Alaska and Canada.

bald eagle

golden eagle

Bald eagles only live in North America. The golden eagle lives in North America, Europe, Asia, and Africa.

Eagle Habitats

As expert hunters, eagles live in places where it's easy to find food. Bald eagles commonly live in forested areas near rivers, lakes, and other large bodies of water, such as **reservoirs**. They've also been seen around **marshes** and coastlines.

Golden eagles' **habitats** are a little different. They mostly live in mountains that are up to 12,000 feet (3,658 m) tall. They also live in **canyons** and along cliffs. They like big areas of open land, too.

> Even though they belong to the same family, bald eagles and golden eagles have different habitats.

Big, Beautiful Birds

There's no mistaking a bald eagle when you see one. Its head is covered in white feathers that make it look "bald." The feathers that cover its body are brown. Its eyes, feet, and beak are yellow. A bald eagle's **wingspan** measures between 6.5 feet (2 m) and 8 feet (2.4 m).

A golden eagle has dark brown feathers on its body and golden feathers on its head and neck. Its wingspan measures between 6 feet (1.8 m) and 7.5 feet (2.3 m). Bald eagles and golden eagles are some of the biggest birds in North America.

RAPTOR FACTOR

Female bald eagles and female golden eagles are usually bigger than males.

Bald eagles have bigger heads than golden eagles. They fly with their wings flat across. Golden eagles have longer tails and fly with their wings slightly raised.

Eagle Eyes

Have you ever heard the term "eagle eyes"? That refers to the bald eagle's eyesight—it's excellent! Bald eagles can spot tiny prey from about 1 mile (1.6 km) away, and they see at least four times better than humans. They mainly eat fish.

When the bald eagle sees its dinner, it can reach speeds of up to 200 miles (322 km) per hour to dive at it. It scoops the prey out of the water with its sharp claws. Then, when it settles down to eat, the bald eagle uses its beak to tear apart the animal's flesh.

A bald eagle mainly eats fish, but it will eat anything that's available, especially in winter. That includes small **mammals**, snakes, turtles, and even dead animals, which are called carrion. Bald eagles are also known to steal food from other birds!

RAPTOR FACTOR

A bald eagle's claws are covered in bumps, which keeps slippery fish from falling through its talons as it flies.

Top Predator

Bald eagles are sometimes thought of as **scavengers**. Golden eagles, on the other hand, are always thought of as predators. This bird hunts by **soaring** high in the sky, but flies low when it's hunting along mountain slopes. It will also **perch** in a high location and search for prey on the ground.

When a golden eagle spots prey, it dives at speeds up to 150 miles (241 km) per hour. The golden eagle's sharp talons help it carry away its catch. Golden eagles eat rabbits, squirrels, birds, lizards, bugs, and sometimes dead animals.

RAPTOR FACTOR

Golden eagles sometimes hunt in pairs.
If prey escapes one of the birds, the other will
swoop in to catch it.

Golden eagles aren't afraid of anything. They've been known to attack large mammals, such as deer, wolves, and caribou.

From the Eagle's Nest

Like most bird species, eagles build nests. They build their nests high in the air. Both bald eagles and golden eagles build nests in tall trees or on cliffs along the sides of mountains. Bald eagle nests are close to water, while golden eagle nests are near where they hunt.

Bald eagles use sticks and twigs to create their nest. Both the male and female help build it. Golden eagles build a nest of sticks and line it with grass, leaves, and other soft plants. Both kinds of eagles use their nest for many years.

Big birds need big nests. The biggest bald eagle nest on record was 9.5 feet (2.9 m) wide and 20 feet (6.1 m) tall! The biggest golden eagle nest on record was 8.5 feet (2.6 m) wide and 20 feet (6.1 m) tall.

golden eagle nest

bald eagle nest

Baby Eagles

Eagles use their nest for laying eggs. Bald eagles lay between two and three eggs at a time. The eggs are white and take about 35 days to hatch. Golden eagles lay around three eggs at a time. The eggs are white with brown markings and take about 45 days to hatch.

Eagle parents must bring babies food, since the young can't fly or hunt yet. Both bald eagle parents hunt. Female golden eagles stay with their babies at first, while the male hunts. Both kinds of baby eagles leave the nest when they're around two or three months old.

Baby eagles look different from their parents at first. Baby golden eagles are white with brown spots. Young bald eagles don't look "bald" yet—the feathers on their head are brown!

RAPTOR FACTOR

Baby eagles are called eaglets.

Majestic Creatures

As the symbol of the United States, the bald eagle stands for strength and freedom. The golden eagle was important to some Native American tribes throughout history. They felt it was strong and had magical powers.

For a long time, bald eagles were in danger of dying out. Laws were passed to protect them, and the number of bald eagles in the wild is growing. There are also laws to protect golden eagles from harm. It's important to respect these **majestic** creatures.

Glossary

bird of prey: A predatory bird that has a hooked beak and sharp talons. Also, another name for a raptor.

canyon: A deep valley between mountains with a river running through it.

habitat: The natural home of a person or animal.

keen: Very strong.

majestic: Having or showing impressive beauty.

mammal: A warm-blooded animal that has a backbone and hair, and feeds milk to its young.

marsh: An area of low-lying land that is flooded and is usually wet throughout the whole year.

perch: To rest in a high location.

reservoir: A large, man-made lake that's used as a source of water.

scavenger: A creature that eats dead animals.

soar: To fly or rise high in the air.

wingspan: The measurement from the tip of one wing to the tip of the other.

Index

B
babies, 20, 21
beaks, 6, 7, 12, 14

C
carnivores, 6
claws, 4, 6, 14, 15

E
eaglets, 21
eggs, 20
eyes, 4, 6, 7, 12, 14

F
feathers, 6, 7,
        12, 20
feet, 6, 12
female, 12, 18, 20

H
habitats, 10

M
male, 12, 18, 20

N
nests, 18, 19, 20

P
prey, 4, 14, 16

S
scavengers, 16
species, 4, 8, 18

T
tail, 13
talons, 6, 7, 15, 16

W
wings, 4, 6, 13
wingspan, 12

Websites

Due to the changing nature of Internet links, PowerKids Press has developed an online list of websites related to the subject of this book. This site is updated regularly. Please use this link to access the list: www.powerkidslinks.com/rapt/eagl